Santa Monica Public Library

I SMP 00 2122807 T

D1164572

MONTANA BRANCH
Santa Monica Public Library
.SEP   2009

The Science of a Loaf of Bread

The Science of Changing Properties

By Andrew Solway

Science and Curriculum Consultant:
Debra Voege, M.A., *Science Curriculum Resource Teacher*

Gareth Stevens
Publishing

Please visit our web site at **www.garethstevens.com**.
For a free color catalog describing Gareth Stevens Publishing's list of high-quality books,
call 1-800-542-2595 (USA) or 1-800-387-3178 (Canada). Gareth Stevens Publishing's fax: 1-877-542-2596

Library of Congress Cataloging-in-Publication Data
Solway, Andrew.
    The science of a loaf of bread : the science of changing properties / by Andrew Solway.
       p. cm. — (The science of ?)
    Includes bibliographical references and index.
    ISBN-10: 1-4339-0043-2   ISBN-13: 978-1-4339-0043-3 (lib. bdg. : alk. paper)
     1. Matter—Properties—Experiments—Juvenile literature. 2. Science—Experiments—Juvenile literature.
   3. Cookery (Bread)—Juvenile literature. 4. Bread—Experiments—Juvenile literature. I. Title.
    QC173.36.S654   2008
    507.8—dc22   2008034031

This North American edition first published in 2009 by
Gareth Stevens Publishing
A Weekly Reader® Company
1 Reader's Digest Road
Pleasantville, NY 10570-7000 USA

This U.S. edition copyright © 2009 by Gareth Stevens, Inc.
Original edition copyright © 2008 by Franklin Watts. First published in Great Britain
in 2008 by Franklin Watts, 338 Euston Road, London NW1 3BH, United Kingdom.

For Discovery Books Limited:
Editor: Rebecca Hunter   Designer: Keith Williams
Illustrator: Stefan Chabluk   Photo researcher: Rachel Tisdale

Gareth Stevens Executive Managing Editor: Lisa M. Herrington
Gareth Stevens Senior Editor: Barbara Bakowski
Gareth Stevens Creative Director: Lisa Donovan
Gareth Stevens Cover Designer: Keith Plechaty
Gareth Stevens Electronic Production Manager: Paul Bodley
Gareth Stevens Publisher: Keith Garton
Special thanks to Laura Anastasia, Michelle Castro, and Jennifer Ryder-Talbot

Photo credits: Shutterstock, cover; istockphoto.com/Jason Alan, p. 4; istockphoto.com/Dmitry Galanternik, p. 5;
istockphoto.com/Vera Bogaerts, p. 6; istockphoto.com/Andrew Penner, p. 7; Corbis/Atlastide Phototravel, p. 9;
Corbis/David Turnley, p. 11 top; istockphoto.com/Vlado Janzekovi, p. 11 bottom; Corbis/Visuals Unlimited, p. 12;
Corbis/Cultura, p. 14; Getty Images/Takako Chiba, p. 15; Getty Images/Neil Corder, p. 16; istockphoto.com, p. 17;
istockphoto.com/Malgorzata Karpas, p. 18; Corbis/Thomas A. Kelly, p. 19; istockphoto.com/Robyn Mackenzie, p. 20;
Shutterstock/H.D. Connelly, p. 21; istockphoto.com/Dr. Heinz Linke, p. 23; Getty Images/Dr. David M. Phillips, p. 25;
istockphoto.com/Michael Neale, p. 26; istockphoto.com/Peter Miller, p. 27; istockphoto.com/Sergei Didyk, p. 28;
istockphoto.com/Alexander Hafemann, p. 29 top; istockphoto.com/Paul Roux, p. 29 bottom. Every effort has been
made to trace copyright holders. We apologize for any inadvertent omissions and would be pleased to insert
appropriate acknowledgments in a subsequent edition.

All rights reserved. No part of this book may be reproduced, stored in a retrieval system, or transmitted in
any form or by any means, electronic, mechanical, photocopying, recording, or otherwise, without the prior
written permission of the copyright holder. For permission, contact **permissions@gspub.com**.

Printed in the United States of America
1 2 3 4 5 6 7 8 9 10 09 08

Contents

Words that appear in **boldface** type are in the glossary on page 30.

Bread Basics

Bread smells wonderful when it is baking—and it tastes delicious when it is baked! Bread has been a **staple food** in many cultures and countries of the world for thousands of years.

▲ *People in countries throughout the world eat different kinds of bread.*

In the Mix

Bread has three main ingredients—flour, **yeast**, and water (with a bit of salt and oil). By themselves, the ingredients are not very tasty. Flour is made by grinding grains, or seeds, of wheat or another **cereal**. Yeast is actually alive! It is a tiny, one-celled organism. Water has no taste of its own.

Magic or Science?

If you mix flour, yeast, and water in the right way and bake the dough, something happens. You get delicious bread!

How does that happen? Is it magic? No, it is science. Read on to find out about the changes that happen between the mixing bowl and the serving plate. Learn about the many different kinds of bread people eat throughout the world. Discover how big bakeries produce thousands of loaves of bread every day. You can even find out what happens to bread after you have eaten it. On pages 8 to 9, there is an easy recipe for making bread that you can try at home. (Caution: Be sure to have an adult help you.)

Happy baking!

What Is a Staple Food?

A staple food is a starchy food that people eat with most meals. In some parts of the world, foods made from wheat are staples. These foods include bread and pasta. In other places, rice is the main staple food. Other examples of staple foods are corn, barley, potatoes, and yams.

▼ *Lentils, beans, rice, and wheat are some examples of staple foods.*

A Slice of Life

Did you eat bread today? Maybe you had toast for breakfast or a sandwich for lunch. Perhaps you had naan or tortillas or a bagel. Maybe you ate a slice of pizza. All of those foods are forms of bread.

Why We Eat Bread

Bread is a staple food, so many people eat a lot of it. We can prepare bread in many ways and use it in a variety of dishes. This staple is inexpensive and widely available, too. Farmers grow wheat in large areas of North America, Europe, and Asia.

Bread provides **nutrients** that our bodies need. It is mainly made up of starch, a **carbohydrate**. Carbohydrates are the main source of energy for the body.

Carbohydrates make up a large part of the **calories** in a well-balanced diet. Bread can fill many of our daily energy needs.

Carbohydrates are not the only nutrients our bodies need. We also need **protein**, fat, and small amounts of **vitamins** and **minerals**.

▼ *In many parts of northern Africa and the Middle East, people cook flatbread over a fire.*

Nutrients Sense

Different kinds of bread have different types of nutrients. White bread is made from white wheat flour. When wheat is ground, the tough parts, known as **bran** and **wheat germ**, are taken out to make white flour. White flour contains plenty of carbohydrates but little protein or fat.

Whole-wheat bread is made from whole-wheat flour. Whole-wheat flour is made from the whole grain, with nothing removed. It contains more protein, vitamins, and other nutrients than white flour. Multigrain breads contain more than one kind of cereal. Breads such as Italian ciabatta have oil or fat in them.

MyPyramid.gov
STEPS TO A HEALTHIER YOU

GRAINS	VEGETABLES	FRUITS
FATS & OILS	MILK	MEAT & BEANS

▲ *This diagram shows the types and proportions of food you should eat daily. The colors represent the five food groups, plus oil. Choose more foods from the food groups with the widest stripes. The person climbing the stairs reminds you to be active every day.*

The Cereal Story

Wheat, rice, corn, barley, oats, rye, millet, and sorghum are cereals. Cereals are types of grass. The part that we eat is the grain, or seed. Grain is often ground into flour but can be used in many other ways, too. Rice grains are usually cooked in water. Oats are steamed and rolled to make oatmeal, a common breakfast food. Corn and rice are sometimes heated until they burst open, to make popcorn or puffed rice.

▼ *Canada is one of the world's biggest producers of wheat.*

Let's Bake Bread!

Does anything taste better than a slice of home-baked bread, warm from the oven? By making your own bread, you can better understand the changes that happen during the process. Here is a simple recipe.
Caution: Be sure to have an adult help you.

What You Need

4 cups (500 grams) white flour
1 teaspoon (5 milliliters) salt
1/4 ounce (7 g) dried fast-action
  yeast
2 tablespoons (30 ml) olive oil
10 ounces (300 ml) warm water
greased baking sheet
3 mixing bowls
wooden spoon

What You Do

First, wash your hands well. You are going to "**knead**" them!

1. Use a wooden spoon to mix the flour, salt, and dried yeast in a bowl. Make a well in the middle of the **mixture**.

2. Mix the oil and water in a separate bowl. Pour the oily water into the well in the flour mixture. Gradually mix, first with the spoon and then with your hands.

3. Remove the dough. Place it on a surface that has been lightly sprinkled with flour. Knead the dough, using the heel of your hand to press down and away from you. Fold the dough over and press it down again.

4. Turn the dough a quarter turn and fold it over again. Keep pressing, folding, and turning for 5 to 10 minutes. The dough should become springy and elastic.

5. Place the dough in a bowl that has been coated with oil. Cover the bowl and leave it in a warm place for about an hour. The bread should rise, doubling in size.

6. Fold and press the risen dough a few times to force the air out. Shape the dough into a ball. Put it on a greased baking sheet. Cut a cross in the top of the dough. Next, leave the dough to rise in a warm place for another hour.

7. Ask an adult to put the loaf in an oven that has been preheated to 425° Fahrenheit (220° Celsius). Bake for 25 to 30 minutes, until browned. Tap the bottom of the pan; it should sound hollow.

8. Leave your loaf to cool for a while on a wire rack. Then cut a slice and take a bite. Delicious!

▼ *The thick walls of a bread baker's oven are made of brick, which holds heat well. The baker puts bread in and takes it out with a long-handled wooden paddle.*

Flour Power

Take a close look at the ingredients that go into a loaf of bread. The most important ingredient is flour. The changes in the flour turn a soggy lump of dough into a crusty loaf of tasty bread.

The Inside Story

A wheat grain is a seed. It has a hard outer **seed coat** to protect against insects in the soil. Inside the grain are two main parts. The **embryo** is the part of the seed that can grow and become a plant. The **endosperm** is a store of food that the embryo can draw on when it starts to grow.

The different parts of the wheat grain are made of different substances. The embryo has a lot of protein. The endosperm contains mostly starch, plus a small amount of protein. The seed coat is made of tough materials that people cannot **digest**.

From Grain to Flour

Today, most flour is made by grinding wheat grains between pairs of rollers. The fine white endosperm is separated from the bran (pieces of the hard seed coat) and the wheat germ (ground-up parts of the embryo). For white flour, only the finely ground endosperm is used. For whole-wheat flour, the larger pieces

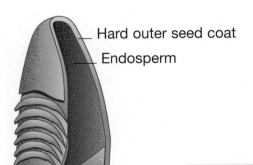

Hard outer seed coat

Endosperm

Embryo

◀ This wheat grain is cut open to show the embryo and endosperm inside.

▲ *The traditional method of grinding flour is to crush the wheat grains with large millstones.*

of bran and wheat germ are rolled again to grind them finer. They are then added to the white flour.

Stone-ground flour is made in a more traditional way, with millstones. These are two disc-shaped stones. One stone is fixed, and the other turns. The grain is fed between the stones through a hole in the center. The grains are crushed and ground into flour. Grooves in the moving stone allow the flour to escape at the outer edge.

Bread Flour

Bread flour has more gluten than other kinds of flour. **Gluten** is a protein. It is the substance that makes bread dough springy and elastic. It also traps the gas bubbles that make bread rise.

▶ *Wheat is a cereal crop. After it is harvested, the grains can be removed and ground into flour.*

Yeast in Action

An important part of making most kinds of bread is letting the dough rise. For this to happen, you need yeast.

Useful Yeast

Yeast is a living thing. It is a type of **fungus**. Mushrooms and molds are other types of fungus. Each yeast cell is shaped like a tiny football. It can be seen only with the aid of a microscope.

Yeasts cannot make their own food. They feed on other substances, particularly sugars and starches. When yeasts have plenty of food (such as the starch in bread flour), they reproduce

▼ *These yeast cells are magnified many times. The cell in the center is budding.*

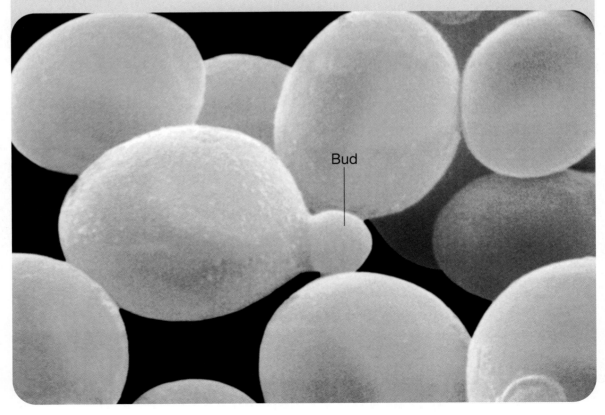

Bud

Fermentation Experimentation

Try this activity to show that growing yeast produces gas. (Caution: Be sure to have an adult help you.)

What You Need
1/4 ounce (7 g) dried fast-action yeast
1 cup (237 ml) hot water
2 tablespoons (30 ml) sugar
2-cup glass measuring cup
spoon
jar that holds 2 cups (474 ml) liquid
small plastic bag
rubber band

What You Do

1. In a measuring cup, mix the yeast, water, and sugar. The mixture will start to bubble.

2. Pour the mixture into a jar.

3. Fasten a plastic bag over the mouth of the jar. Secure it with a rubber band. Make sure the seal is tight so that there is no leakage.

4. Watch what happens. The plastic bag will fill up with gas made by the yeast mixture.

rapidly. In a process called **budding**, the yeast forms a growth called a bud. It breaks off and becomes a new cell.

As yeasts break down their food, they produce waste products. These include alcohol and the gas **carbon dioxide**. This process is called **fermentation**. The carbon dioxide becomes trapped in tiny pockets within the dough and makes it rise.

Yeast also adds to the flavor of bread. Yeasts have proteins called **enzymes**. The enzymes break down the starch in flour into other, simpler substances. These include weak **acids** (like the acids in apple juice). These simple chemicals give the baked bread a better flavor than that of raw flour.

Yeast Is Everywhere!

Yeasts exist almost everywhere in nature, including in the air. Using yeast to make bread rise was probably an accidental discovery. Perhaps a cook made dough and set it aside for a while. Yeast that had gotten into the dough naturally could have made it rise.

From Flour to Dough

You now know all about flour and yeast, two of the main ingredients in bread. It's time to find out what happens when you are rolling in dough!

Proof Positive

Before baking with yeast, you may want to make sure that the yeast is alive. Testing to see if yeast is active is called proofing. First, stir a tablespoon of sugar into about a half cup of warm water. Then stir in a packet of yeast. Set aside the mixture for 10 minutes. If the yeast is working properly, bubbles form as carbon dioxide is produced. A creamy foam appears on the surface of the liquid.

Getting Wet

Dried yeast and flour can be stored for months in a cool, dark place. Adding water to the flour and yeast starts the bread-making process. Changes happen quickly!

You have already learned that adding warm water to yeast causes the yeast cells to grow and divide. What changes happen to the flour? First, the starch in the flour soaks up water and swells. Second, two kinds of protein in the flour begin to connect to form another kind of protein—gluten.

Need to Knead?

It is possible to make bread without kneading the dough.

Great Balls of Gluten

Take a piece of dough made with bread flour and form it into a ball. Squeeze the dough gently as you hold it under a slow stream of water. The starch in the dough is washed away, leaving a ball of elastic, springy gluten.

However, kneading helps in two ways. First, kneading mixes the ingredients thoroughly so that the dough has no lumps or holes. Second, kneading speeds up the process of forming the stretchy gluten.

Well-kneaded dough is strong and can easily be formed into different shapes. Try making a braided loaf of bread. Split your dough into three equal pieces. Roll each piece out to form a long, fat rope. Then braid the three ropes to make a loaf.

◀ *The gluten in flour helps make dough stretchy and flexible. Without gluten, this baker would not be able to stretch pizza dough into a thin, round crust.*

▲ *Many cooks in Japan and China use gluten. They may deep-fry or steam it. They also use gluten to make some kinds of* wagashi, *or Japanese sweets (above).*

On the Rise

You know what makes bread rise. It is carbon dioxide gas made by the yeast in the dough. Letting the dough rise makes the bread light and fluffy. The conditions must be just right, though, for the dough to rise properly.

How Dough Grows

It is important that the yeast cells grow quickly while bread is being made. That is brought about by adding warm water to the dough and putting it in a warm place to rise. When yeast cells are warm, they grow quickly. As a result, they produce more carbon dioxide, and the bread rises fast. The water must be the right temperature—about 100° F (38° C). Boiling water would kill the yeast, and the bread would not rise.

Yeast will still grow, and bread will still rise, at a lower temperature. If you leave dough in a refrigerator overnight, it will rise as much as it does in an hour in a warm place. But if the dough is kept warm for a time and then becomes cold, the gas that is trapped inside it will shrink. The dough will sink.

▲ *When dough rises, it fills with bubbles of carbon dioxide gas. The dough grows larger and takes up more space.*

No-Yeast Bread

Have you ever heard of **unleavened** bread? It is flatbread, made without yeast. Naan, pita, and injera are three types of unleavened bread. People in different parts of the world make many varieties of flatbread.

Bakers sometimes use ingredients other than yeast to make bread rise. You can find out more about those methods on pages 20 to 21.

▲ *A gas burner heats the air inside a hot-air balloon. As the heated air expands, the balloon rises because the hot air is less **dense** than the surrounding cool air. Carbon dioxide also expands as it becomes warmer. The carbon dioxide produced by yeast in bread dough causes the dough to rise as it is heated.*

Changing Gases

Like yeast, the carbon dioxide produced when bread rises is affected by temperature. The amount of space a gas takes up depends on its temperature. As a gas becomes warmer, it expands, or takes up more space. As the gas cools, it contracts, or takes up less space. You can demonstrate this change by doing a simple experiment. First, blow up a balloon. Use a tape measure or a string to measure around the balloon at its widest part. Put the balloon in a refrigerator for about an hour. Then remove the balloon and measure it again. You will find that the balloon has shrunk! Can you explain why?

Into the Oven

Once dough has been kneaded and has risen, it is ready to go into the oven. What kinds of changes happen during baking?

Turn Up the Heat

When you put bread dough in the oven, it gets hot. The gases trapped inside the bread get hot, too. As they heat up, they expand. The dough becomes larger. At first, the yeast in the dough grows more quickly. But when the yeast gets very hot, it no longer makes carbon dioxide.

Heat also dries out the bread. Some of the water in the dough **evaporates**, or turns from a liquid into a gas. Other substances in the bread, such as alcohol, evaporate, too. These changes affect the taste of the bread.

Browning reactions change the outside of the bread, which becomes harder and darker. These reactions occur when a carbohydrate reacts with a protein at very high temperatures. Browning reactions also affect bread flavor.

◀ *The outside of this loaf of bread is crusty because of browning reactions during baking. The inside of the loaf is soft and chewy.*

▲ *Bagels are cooked to golden-brown perfection at this bakery in New York City.*

The Upper Crust

Bread is always baked at a high temperature. High heat cooks the outside of the bread quickly, forming a brown, crunchy crust. Yet the inside of the loaf remains soft and springy.

The bread would take longer to bake at a lower temperature. The crust would be thick, and the inside of the loaf would become tough and hard.

Bread Ovens

Professional bakers use ovens that are different from the oven you probably have in your home. A bread oven has thick walls that hold heat well. The oven takes a long time to heat up, but it stays hot for a long time, too. This means that the oven does not lose much heat when it is opened.

Most bread ovens are steam ovens. Steam, or water vapor, is forced into the oven while the bread bakes. Steam ovens produce a good crust on breads.

No Baker's Yeast

Most bakers today use dried yeast that comes in a package. Sourdough bread and soda bread are made without baker's yeast. Sourdough bread uses a mixture of **microbes**. Soda bread rises because of a different type of chemical reaction.

A Tangy Taste

Wild yeasts and other microbes occur naturally in the air and in grains. Wild yeast can be used to make a **starter**, a mixture that is used to make bread rise.

Starter dough can be made by mixing flour with water, covering it with a cloth, and letting it stand for several days. Microbes grow in the mixture. Some of them are wild yeasts. The yeasts produce carbon dioxide. The other microbes in the starter dough are **bacteria**. They produce a weak acid, which gives sourdough bread its slightly tangy taste.

The dough is refreshed a few times by adding more flour and

◀ *Sourdough bread is made with wild yeast kept alive in a starter dough. The starter gives the bread its unique taste.*

water. Within about five days, the starter dough has the right balance of microbes.

Baking Soda and Buttermilk

Soda bread can be prepared quickly. Instead of yeast, a combination of baking soda and buttermilk makes the bread rise. Bakers mix the baking soda and buttermilk with flour, water, and salt to make the dough. The buttermilk is acidic. When it combines with the baking soda, a chemical reaction takes place. One of the products of the reaction is carbon dioxide, which makes the soda bread rise.

▶ *Soda bread rises without the use of yeast. Bakers sometimes add ingredients such as raisins and nuts to the dough.*

Buttermilk

Traditional buttermilk is the liquid left over after cream is churned to make butter. Today, most buttermilk is made by adding special bacteria to cow's milk. The bacteria produce acid, which gives buttermilk a sour taste.

Irish Soda Bread

Soda bread is a popular food in Ireland. The kind of wheat that is used in traditional bread making does not grow well in Ireland's climate. Irish bakers began to make soda bread when baking soda was introduced to the country in the mid-1800s. At first, soda bread contained only flour, buttermilk, baking soda, and salt.

Bread on a Big Scale

Commercial bakeries turn out thousands of loaves of bread daily. In 2007, the revenue of U.S. commercial bakeries was $28 billion. That's a lot of dough!

Making the Dough

First, the yeast, the water, and about three-fourths of the flour are mixed together. They form a soft mixture called a **sponge**. The sponge then sits in a warm room for a few hours, until it stops rising and begins to fall. Next, the rest of the flour is mixed in to make

Making Bread in a Commercial Bakery

Water, yeast, and ¾ flour

Sponge

Remaining flour added

Dough left to rise

Mixing dough

First proofing

Rounding

Dividing

Molding

Panning

Second proofing

Baking

Depanning

▶ *Huge amounts of dough are mixed in a commercial bakery.*

the dough. It goes back to the warm room to rise again.

Shaping the Dough

The finished dough goes through a dividing machine that cuts it into loaf-sized pieces. Another machine shapes the dough pieces into round balls (rounding). By this time, the dough has lost some of its gas bubbles and elasticity. It is left to rest for a few minutes (first proofing stage) and then molded into shapes and put into pans. The dough rises for another 20 minutes (second proofing) before being baked.

Baking the Dough

Commercial bread ovens have a continuous line of loaves moving through them. Tunnel ovens have a conveyor belt that takes the loaves through a long, hot tunnel. Chamber ovens also have a conveyor belt. It carries the loaves through a heated chamber.

As the baked loaves come out of the oven, they are removed from the pans. The loaves are then cooled on racks before being packed and shipped to stores.

Bread Additives

Bread that is made commercially has to keep longer than homemade bread. The dough must come out right every time. A baker cannot afford to throw away a ton of dough because it has not risen properly!

To help bread stay fresh and come out well every time, bakers add small amounts of chemicals to the bread. For instance, some **additives** stop bread from going stale quickly. They are called preservatives. Other additives ensure that the dough rises well.

Bread is shipped to markets that may be thousands of miles from the bakery. Additives help keep food appealing. They may improve taste, texture, or color.

In Your Breadbasket

What is the best part of baking bread? Eating the results! When you eat a slice of bread, you chew and then swallow. After that, you may not think about the bread anymore. But it has just begun a long journey through your **digestive tract**.

Break It Down

Bread is made up mainly of carbohydrates, proteins, and a small amount of fat. The human body cannot use those complex substances directly. The body must break them down into simpler nutrients that are absorbed into the blood. The nutrients are then carried to all parts of the body.

Bread in Your Body

The digestion of bread starts in the mouth, with the action of **saliva**. Saliva contains an enzyme that begins to break down the starch into sugars.

After bread has been chewed and swallowed, it is pushed through the esophagus. The esophagus is a tube that connects the throat and the stomach. The stomach is a hollow organ where food is stored

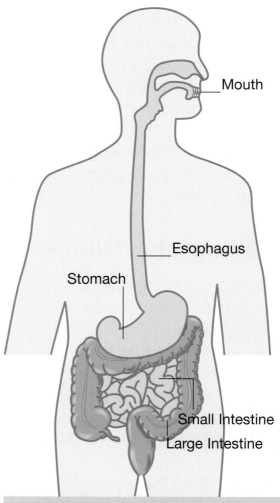

Mouth

Esophagus

Stomach

Small Intestine

Large Intestine

▲ *Bread and other foods are broken down as they pass through the digestive tract.*

and mixed. The swallowed food mixes with acid and other liquids. The proteins in the bread start to break down.

From the stomach, the mixed food goes into a long tube called the small intestine. In the first part of the small intestine, proteins, carbohydrates, and fats are broken down into useful nutrients. In the second part of the small intestine, the nutrients are absorbed into the blood.

The last stage of digestion happens in the large intestine. This tube is wider than the small intestine. The bran and other parts of bread that people cannot digest go into the large intestine. Water is absorbed from the waste. Solid waste materials are passed out of the body in a bowel movement.

Fiber

Foods such as whole-wheat bread and brown rice are rich in **fiber**. Fiber is a kind of carbohydrate that the human body cannot break down into nutrients. It helps the digestive system work properly. Fiber also helps lower the risk for certain diseases and helps control weight.

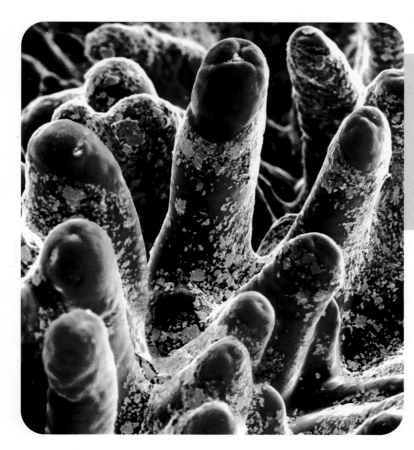

◀ Tiny, finger-like *villi* cover the inside of the small intestine. The villi (as seen here through a microscope) absorb nutrients.

Physical Changes

In science, there are two types of changes: **physical changes** and **chemical changes**. Physical changes can be reversed, but chemical changes cannot. Bread making involves both types of changes.

Sifting

When the dry ingredients of bread are stirred together, they form a mixture. The baker combines the ingredients but can separate them again. The mixing of solid ingredients is a physical change. It is reversible.

There are several ways to separate mixtures. The easiest way to separate solids is to sift them. Flour, salt, and yeast can be separated in this way. Grains of flour can pass through a sieve with small holes, but yeast and salt cannot. A sieve with slightly larger holes can separate the yeast from the salt.

Filtering

Filtering is a way of separating solids from liquids. The solid particles are usually smaller, so the sieve has smaller holes.

A coffee maker mixes ground coffee beans and hot water. Some of the coffee **dissolves** in the water, giving it flavor. To get rid of the bits of ground coffee that don't dissolve, the liquid is poured through a paper filter.

◀ *Some solids can be separated by sifting them.*

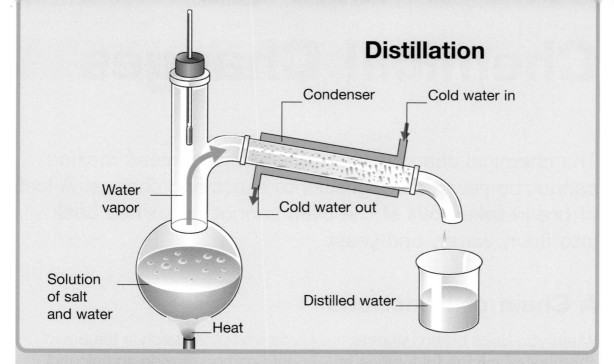

Distillation

Condenser · Cold water in

Water vapor

Cold water out

Solution of salt and water

Heat

Distilled water

▲ *Distillation is a process that can be used to separate a solution of salt and water.*

Distilling

A **solution** results when a solid dissolves in a liquid. You can no longer see the solid. You might think the change cannot be reversed. But even this mixture can be separated. For example, it is possible to separate a solution of salt and water through the process of **distillation**. The solution is heated until it boils. The water evaporates, turning from a liquid into water vapor. Then the water is cooled so that it **condenses**, or changes from a gas back into a liquid. The liquid water is collected, and solid salt crystals remain.

Top of the Tower

A special kind of distillation, called fractional distillation, is used at oil refineries. There, **crude oil** is separated into gasoline and other useful substances. The process of refining oil starts at a distillation tower, like the one shown below.

27

Chemical Changes

The chemical changes that occur during bread making cannot be reversed. Ingredients react and change. A loaf of bread taken out of the oven cannot be turned back into flour, water, and yeast.

A Chain of Reactions

When you bake bread, several chemical reactions take place at the same time. First, two proteins in the flour combine chemically to make gluten. There is no gluten in the flour. But when the flour is mixed with water and kneaded, gluten forms.

The yeast in the bread also sets off some chemical reactions. It converts the starch in the bread into carbon dioxide and alcohol. The carbon dioxide gas makes the bread rise and gives it a spongy texture. When the dough is baked at a high temperature, the yeast is killed, and those chemical reactions stop.

Where's the Fire?

You are probably familiar with another chemical reaction—combustion, or burning. Many different materials burn, but all combustion involves the same kind of chemical reaction. Most materials that burn, such as paper, wood, coal, oil, and

◄ Heat causes chemical changes in foods during cooking.

▲ *Rusting is a slower chemical reaction than burning. Over time, iron gradually reacts with oxygen in the air to form iron oxide, or rust.*

gasoline, contain a lot of **carbon**. The carbon combines with oxygen from the air to produce carbon dioxide. Combustion often releases energy as heat or light.

▼ *If you leave bread in the toaster too long, you might cause too much combustion!*

Slow Reaction Time

Many chemical reactions go on around us. Some are slow and simple, such as the rusting of iron. It is caused by a single chemical reaction between the iron and oxygen in the air. The reaction produces iron oxide, commonly called rust. It can take weeks or months for a piece of iron to rust.

Glossary

acids: chemical compounds with certain similar properties. Some acids are essential for life.

additives: chemicals added to keep food fresh or to improve its flavor, color, or texture

bacteria: tiny, single-cell organisms that sometimes cause disease

bran: the edible broken seed coats of cereal grain

browning reactions: chemical reactions that produce the flavors and brown color of many cooked foods, including bread

budding: development of an organism from a bud, or outgrowth

calories: a unit of energy supplied by food

carbohydrate: a kind of nutrient. Sugars and starches are carbohydrates.

carbon: a common chemical element in all plants and animals

carbon dioxide: a gas in the air

cereal: a grass-like plant, such as rice, wheat, or oats, whose seeds are used as food

chemical changes: changes that happen when substances become new or different products

condenses: changes from a gas to a liquid or solid

crude oil: a substance found in the ground that is used to make fuels, plastics, paints, and other products

dense: closely packed together

digest: to break down food chemically into simple nutrients that the body can absorb and use

digestive tract: organs that break down food into smaller particles for use in the human body

dissolves: mixes completely with a solid, liquid, or gas

distillation: purifying a substance by heating it and condensing the vapor given off

embryo: an undeveloped plant within a seed

endosperm: nourishment for the embryo of a plant

enzymes: proteins that speed up chemical reactions in the body

evaporates: changes from a liquid or solid into a gas

fermentation: the chemical breakdown of a substance using yeasts or other microbes

fiber: food material that the body cannot digest

fungus: a plant-like living thing such as a mold or yeast

gluten: the tough, sticky substance that remains in flour when the starch is taken out

knead: to press and squeeze dough with the hands

microbes: organisms too small to be seen without a microscope

minerals: chemicals, such as calcium and iron, that are needed in small amounts by the body

mixture: substances that are mixed but not chemically combined

nutrients: substances that the body needs to survive and grow

physical changes: changes of matter from one form to another without creating new substances

protein: a complex chemical that is a necessary part of the cells of animals and plants

saliva: liquid made in the mouth that starts digestion of starch

seed coat: a seed's outer covering

solution: a mixture formed by a substance dissolved in a liquid

sponge: a soft mixture of yeast, liquid, and flour that is allowed to rise and then mixed with other ingredients to create bread dough

staple food: a starchy food, such as bread, rice, or potatoes, that is a major part of the diet

starter: material containing yeast used to bring about fermentation

unleavened: made without yeast

villi: small, finger-like projections that line the small intestine

vitamins: substances found in food that the body needs in small amounts to be healthy

wheat germ: the embryo in a wheat grain

yeast: tiny, single-cell plants that grow quickly and make dough rise

Find Out More

Explore the Science of Yeast
www.lesaffreyeastcorp.com/SoY/ students.html
Find plenty of yeast facts, history, experiments, and images.

Science of Cooking: Bread
www.exploratorium.edu/ cooking/bread
Learn about the science of baking and try some experiments.

Publisher's note to educators and parents: Our editors have carefully reviewed these web sites to ensure that they are suitable for children. Many web sites change frequently, however, and we cannot guarantee that a site's future contents will continue to meet our high standards of quality and educational value. Be advised that children should be closely supervised whenever they access the Internet.

Index